Effective Carbon Rates 2021

PRICING CARBON EMISSIONS THROUGH TAXES AND EMISSIONS TRADING

OECD

BETTER POLICIES FOR BETTER LIVES

This document, as well as any data and map included herein, are without prejudice to the status of or sovereignty over any territory, to the delimitation of international frontiers and boundaries and to the name of any territory, city or area.

The statistical data for Israel are supplied by and under the responsibility of the relevant Israeli authorities. The use of such data by the OECD is without prejudice to the status of the Golan Heights, East Jerusalem and Israeli settlements in the West Bank under the terms of international law.

Please cite this publication as:
OECD (2021), *Effective Carbon Rates 2021: Pricing Carbon Emissions through Taxes and Emissions Trading*, OECD Publishing, Paris, *https://doi.org/10.1787/0e8e24f5-en*.

ISBN 978-92-64-35891-1 (print)
ISBN 978-92-64-85463-5 (pdf)

Foreword

This report was prepared by the Tax Policy and Statistics division in the OECD's Centre for Tax Policy and Administration under the auspices of the Committee on Fiscal Affairs and the Environment Policy Committee. It is unique in its comprehensive approach, integrating carbon prices that result from taxes and emissions trading systems into effective carbon rates.

The report highlights key results of the update to 2018 of the *Effective Carbon Rates* database, which can be assessed in its full detail for 44 OECD and G20 countries via OECD.STAT. The database on OECD.STAT also provides effective carbon rates for 2012 and 2015.

In addition, the report provides estimates of the impact of higher permit prices and recent as well as likely future reforms of emissions trading systems in China and in the European Union.

The report was drafted by Florens Flues and Kurt Van Dender. The database architecture was developed originally by Luisa Dressler and Florens Flues and has been updated by Florens Flues and Konstantinos Theodoropoulos. Information on carbon prices that result from taxes has been obtained from the OECD's Taxing Energy Use database, which has recently been updated by Jonas Teusch and Konstantinos Theodoropoulos. Information on emissions trading systems was collected and processed by Florens Flues and Konstantinos Theodoropoulos. Karena Garnier, Hazel Healy, Natalie Lagorce and Carrie Tyler improved the presentation and the dissemination of the work. Michael Sharratt advised on graphical design and web-presentation. Marie-Aurélie Elkurd typeset the report. All contributors are in the OECD's Centre for Tax Policy and Administration.

The authors would like to thank their colleagues Nils Axel Braathen, David Bradbury, Luisa Dressler, Jonas Teusch and Konstantinos Theodoropoulos from the OECD for their very insightful feedback on earlier versions of the report.

The report was discussed by the OECD's Joint Meetings of Tax and Environment Experts, and it was approved for declassification by the Committee on Fiscal Affairs and the Environment Policy Committee. The authors would like to thank in particular the delegates to the Joint Meetings and their colleagues in supranational, national and subnational government administrations for their assistance with the provision of data, as well as for invaluable suggestions, inputs and comments received at various stages of preparing the data and the report.

Table of contents

Tables

Figures

Boxes

Executive Summary

In the past few decades, heat waves have become hotter, storms more severe, and droughts drier. Extreme weather events occur more often and are more severe because temperatures are rising. The increase in temperatures is the consequence of greenhouse gas emissions, including the carbon emissions from fuel combustion. These gases create a greenhouse effect by which the planet overheats, slowly but constantly. We fuel climate change by burning high carbon fuels.

Left unchecked, climate change will have dire consequences, much worse than what we are beginning to experience. However, by reducing greenhouse gas emissions decisively and phasing them out eventually, countries can stabilise the climate and manage its impact on economies, improving at the same time air and water quality. There are many ways to achieve this, for example renewable energy, green hydrogen and zero-carbon building material, and being more mindful with carbon-intensive activities.

Carbon pricing encourages the required shift of production and consumption decisions towards low and zero carbon options very effectively. Based on data from earlier OECD publications on Taxing Energy Use and Effective Carbon Rates a well-published academic paper finds that an increase of the ECR by EUR 10 per tonne CO_2 reduces emission by 7.3% on average over time. Recent increases in the ECR in the United Kingdom´s electricity sector, as well as in the European Union Emissions Trading System (EU ETS) were also accompanied by a strong decline in emissions. There are also other policy instruments, but carbon pricing is very important, because it creates strong incentives by itself and because it increases coherence across climate policy packages.

This study highlights how 44 OECD and G20 countries, which together account for about 80% of global carbon emissions from energy use, price carbon emissions from energy use. Specifically, it describes *Effective carbon rates* (ECRs), which summarise how countries price carbon through fuel excise taxes, carbon taxes and emissions trading systems.

In each of the 44 countries, the ECRs are measured for six economic sectors: industry, electricity generation, residential and commercial energy use, road transport, off-road transport, and agriculture and fisheries. The report highlights the structure of effective carbon rates across countries and sectors in 2018 and discusses change compared to 2012 and 2015. Detailed information on ECRs by country and sector for the years 2018, 2015 and 2012 is available on OECD.STAT. The report also provides an assessment of major developments since 2018, namely the impact of more ambitious emissions trading in China and the EU.

The report discusses progress with carbon pricing against three benchmarks. The first benchmark, EUR 30 per tonne of CO_2, is an historic low-end price benchmark of carbon costs and a minimum price level to start triggering meaningful abatement efforts. The second benchmark, EUR 60 per tonne of CO_2, is a forward looking 2030 low-end and mid-range 2020 benchmark. The third benchmark, EUR 120 per tonne of CO_2, is a central estimate of the carbon costs in 2030. For the presentation of key results, the report focuses on the EUR 60 per tonne CO_2 benchmark. The Effective Carbon Rates database on OECD.STAT shows results for all three carbon pricing benchmarks.

The *Carbon Pricing Score (CPS)* answers the question of how far countries have attained the goal of pricing all energy related carbon emissions at the three benchmarks for carbon costs or more. The more progress a country has made towards the relevant benchmark value, the higher the CPS. For example, a CPS of 100% against a EUR 60 per tonne CO_2 benchmark (CPS_{60}) means that a country or the group of countries prices all carbon emissions from energy use at EUR 60 or more. A CPS of 0% means that the country prices no emissions at all. An intermediate CPS between 0% and 100% means that some emissions are priced, but that not all emissions are priced at a level that equals or exceeds the benchmark.

Key findings

Overall progress with carbon pricing remains modest

- Around 60% of carbon emissions from energy use in OECD and G20 countries remained entirely unpriced in 2018.
- The 44 OECD and G20 countries together have not even reached a fifth of the goal to price all emissions at least at EUR 60 per tonne CO_2 (i.e. the CPS_{60}) in 2018.
- Less than a quarter of the countries studied are more than halfway to the EUR 60 benchmark, and just three countries achieved more than two-thirds of the benchmark in 2018.

Progress between 2015 and 2018 differs across countries

- A number of countries improved their carbon pricing performance significantly. For example, the top ten performing countries in 2018 progressed by around 6 percentage points towards the EUR 60 benchmark.
- By contrast, the ten countries that scored lowest in terms of the EUR 60 benchmark in 2018 showed no improvement since 2015.

Carbon pricing performance varies across sectors

- Effective carbon rates are particularly low in the electricity and the industry sectors.
- In the residential and commercial sector, there is significant heterogeneity, where a handful of countries are 70% along the way towards pricing all carbon emissions at EUR 60 per tonne of CO_2 or more, but with very low carbon prices in other countries.

Fuel excise taxes dominate effective carbon rates

- Across countries, taxes represent 93% of the overall effective marginal carbon rates and emissions trading systems account for 7%. Fuel excise taxes, which usually are not primarily motivated by climate objectives, account for 89% of effective marginal rates. Carbon taxes represent only 4%.
- Accounting for free allocation of emission permits in emissions trading systems, emission permits only contributed 3% of the effective average carbon rate.

Conclusions

Countries that increase their carbon pricing scores improve alignment of carbon prices with the costs of emissions to society and move towards a greener growth path

While no country has yet reached the goal to price all its carbon emissions at low-end estimates of carbon costs, countries with higher carbon pricing scores are more carbon efficient. In addition, countries that increase their carbon pricing scores also become more carbon efficient.

1 Introduction

This chapter defines effective carbon rates and provides context. Effective carbon rates are the total price that applies to carbon dioxide emissions from energy use as a result of market-based instruments (fuel excise taxes, carbon taxes and carbon emission permit prices). The report measures effective carbon rates from energy use for 44 OECD and G20 countries, which together account for about 80% of global carbon emissions from energy use.

The Effective Carbon Rates (ECRs) database is the most detailed and most comprehensive account currently available of how 44 OECD and G20 countries – responsible for around 80% of global carbon emissions – price carbon emissions from energy use. The ECR is the sum of taxes and tradeable permits that effectively put a price on carbon emissions.

The 2021 edition of Effective Carbon Rates shows how the 44 countries priced carbon emissions in 2012, 2015 and 2018 and evaluates progress over this period. It also shows how the three different components of the ECR – fuel excise taxes, carbon taxes and tradeable carbon emission permits (see Figure 1.1) – contribute to the overall carbon price. Irrespective of the policy objectives for their introduction, all three components of the ECR are defined over a tax base that either is CO_2-emissions or is directly proportional to them (e.g., litres of diesel, or tonnes of coal). The three components each make low- and zero- carbon energy more competitive by increasing the price of high-carbon alternatives, encouraging energy users to curtail their use of high carbon energy and switch to low- or zero-carbon options.

Figure 1.1. Components of the Effective Carbon Rate

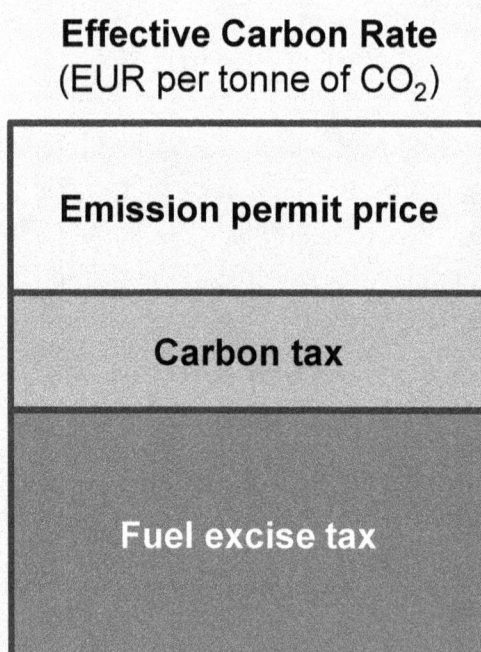

Effective Carbon Rate
(EUR per tonne of CO_2)

Emission permit price

Carbon tax

Fuel excise tax

Data on emission permit prices and their coverage is originally gathered for the Effective Carbon Rates database and data on carbon taxes and fuel excise taxes is taken from the Taxing Energy Use database (OECD, 2019[1]). The first publication of Effective Carbon Rates describes the methodology for matching permit prices with taxes (OECD, 2016[2]).

In line with previous editions of Taxing Energy Use (OECD, 2013[3]; OECD, 2015[4]; OECD, 2018[5]; OECD, 2019[1]), as well as Effective Carbon Rates (OECD, 2016[2]; OECD, 2018[6]) this publication reports results including emissions from the combustion of biomass. Results excluding emissions from the combustion of biomass are available via the Effective Carbon Rates database on OECD.STAT. Annex 3.A of Effective

Carbon Rates 2018 (OECD, 2018[6]) discusses the implications of the combustion approach and considers evidence on lifecycle emissions of biofuels. It also discusses why emission bases from Taxing Energy Use and Effective Carbon Rates are not directly comparable with UNFCCC inventories.

References

OECD (2019), *Taxing Energy Use 2019: Using Taxes for Climate Action*, OECD Publishing, Paris, https://dx.doi.org/10.1787/058ca239-en.   [1]

OECD (2018), *Effective Carbon Rates 2018. Pricing Carbon Emissions Through Taxes and Emissions Trading*, OECD Publishing, Paris, https://doi.org/10.1787/9789264305304-en.   [6]

OECD (2018), *Taxing Energy Use 2018: Companion to the Taxing Energy Use Database*, OECD Publishing, Paris.   [5]

OECD (2016), *Effective Carbon Rates: Pricing CO2 through Taxes and Emissions Trading Systems*, OECD Publishing, Paris, https://dx.doi.org/10.1787/9789264260115-en.   [2]

OECD (2015), *Taxing Energy Use 2015: OECD and Selected Partner Economies*, OECD Publishing, Paris, https://dx.doi.org/10.1787/9789264232334-en.   [4]

OECD (2013), *Taxing Energy Use: A Graphical Analysis*, OECD Publishing, Paris, https://dx.doi.org/10.1787/9789264183933-en.   [3]

2 Carbon pricing works

This chapter sheds light on the role of carbon pricing as a key decarbonisation policy. It provides a general estimate of how strongly carbon prices reduce emissions. In addition, the chapter describes two practical examples of significant increases in effective carbon rates that were soon followed by a strong decline in emissions: First, the carbon price support in the United Kingdom, then the increase in emission permit prices in the European Union Emissions Trading System between 2018 and 2019.

Carbon pricing is a very effective decarbonisation policy. Carbon prices make low- and zero- carbon energy more competitive compared to high-carbon alternatives, and reduce emissions. Carbon prices encourage emitters to find and use economical ways of cutting emissions. By increasing the price of high-carbon energy, carbon prices reduce demand for carbon-intensive fuels (Arlinghaus (2015[7]); Martin et al. (2016[8]). In addition, strong commitment to carbon prices creates certainty for investors that it pays to invest in the use of available zero- and low-carbon technologies and the development of new ones.

Using OECD (2013[3]; 2016[2]) data, Sen and Vollebergh (2018[9]) estimate that a EUR 1 increase in the *effective carbon rate* leads to a 0.73% reduction in emissions over time. This means that, for a country that starts from no carbon price at all, the introduction of a carbon tax of EUR 10 per tonne of CO_2 on its entire energy base would be expected reduce emissions by an estimated 7.3%.[1]

One practical example is the carbon price support in the United Kingdom, which increased effective carbon rates in the electricity sector from EUR 7 per tonne CO_2 to more than EUR 36 between 2012 and 2018. Emissions in the electricity sector in the country fell by 73% in the same period (UK Department for Business, 2020[10]), showing a strong response of UK utilities to higher effective carbon rates.[2] The higher carbon rates in the electricity sector made it profitable for utilities to replace coal with natural gas, which is about half as emission-intensive as coal per unit of energy, and zero-carbon renewables. Overall CO_2-emissions in the United Kingdom decreased by 27% of which 24 percentage points were due to cleaner electricity generation (UK Department for Business, 2020[11]).

Another practical example concerns the European Union Emissions Trading System (EU ETS). From 2018 to 2019, permit prices in the EU ETS increased by EUR 8.90 per tonne CO_2, from about EUR 16 to EUR 25 (ICAP, 2020[12]). At the same time, overall emissions in the EU ETS decreased by 8.9% (Marcu et al., 2020[13]), illustrating a significant short-term response of emitters covered by the EU ETS to higher permit prices.[3] The emission decrease was particularly strong for the electricity generation sector with 13.9% (Marcu et al., 2020[13]). Owners of power plants have to buy emission permits for all emissions of their plants. In the industry sector, where the vast majority of emission permits is allocated to facilities for free, emissions fell by 1.8% (Marcu et al., 2020[13]). Free permit allocation implies that the *effective average carbon rate* that accounts for free allocation, and which is decisive for the ranking of investment projects with similar outputs but different carbon-intensities, is substantially lower than the *effective marginal carbon rate* that does not take the amount of free allocation into account (see Box 4.1 for a more in-depth explanation).

References

Arlinghaus, J. (2015), "Impacts of Carbon Prices on Indicators of Competitiveness: A Review of Empirical Findings", *OECD Environment Working Papers*, No. 87, OECD Publishing, Paris, http://dx.doi.org/10.1787/5js37p21grzq-en.   [1]

ICAP (2020), *International Carbon Action Partnership (ICAP) - ETS Prices*, https://icapcarbonaction.com/en/ets-prices (accessed on 13 October 2020).   [8]

Marcu, A. et al. (2020), *2020 State of the EU ETS Report*, ERCST, Wegener Center, BloombergNEF and Ecoact.   [9]

Martin, R., M. Muûls and U. Wagner (2016), "The Impact of the European Union Emissions Trading Scheme on Regulated Firms: What Is the Evidence after Ten Years?", *Review of Environmental Economics and Policy*, Vol. 10/1, pp. 129-148, http://dx.doi.org/10.1093/reep/rev016.   [2]

OECD (2016), *Effective Carbon Rates: Pricing CO2 through Taxes and Emissions Trading Systems*, OECD Publishing, Paris, https://dx.doi.org/10.1787/9789264260115-en. [4]

OECD (2013), *Taxing Energy Use: A Graphical Analysis*, OECD Publishing, Paris, https://dx.doi.org/10.1787/9789264183933-en. [3]

Perino, G., R. Ritz and A. van Benthem (2019), "Understanding Overlapping Policies: Internal Carbon Leakage and the Punctured Waterbed", *NBER Working Paper Series*, No. 25643, NBER, Cambridge, http://www.nber.org/papers/w25643.ack (accessed on 11 April 2019). [10]

Sen, S. and H. Vollebergh (2018), "The effectiveness of taxing the carbon content of energy consumption", *Journal of Environmental Economics and Management*, Vol. 92, pp. 74-99, http://dx.doi.org/10.1016/J.JEEM.2018.08.017. [5]

UK Department for Business, E. (2020), *Digest of UK Energy Statistics (DUKES) 2020*, UK Department for Business, Energy & Industrial Strategy, https://www.gov.uk/government/statistics/digest-of-uk-energy-statistics-dukes-2020 (accessed on 13 October 2020). [7]

UK Department for Business, E. (2020), *Updated energy and emissions projections: 2018 - Projections of greenhouse gas emissions and energy demand from 2018 to 2035.*, UK Department for Business, Energy & Industrial Strategy, https://www.gov.uk/government/publications/updated-energy-and-emissions-projections-2018 (accessed on 13 October 2020). [6]

Notes

[1] The new tax will increase the price of carbon-intensive fuel, but at a level of EUR 10 per tonne of CO_2 the overall price increase is moderate. For example, heating oil prices will increase by about 4%, assuming that the country also levies a standard VAT rate of 15% on energy products and that pre-tax heating fuel prices correspond to average levels in the EU 28 as of 26 November 2018.

[2] While the higher effective carbon rates reduced emissions in the United Kingdom, some of these additional emission reductions may have been counteracted by an increase in emissions in other countries that are part of the European Union Emissions Trading System (EU ETS). However, limited transmission capacity between the United Kingdom´s and the European Mainland´s electricity grids puts a limit on simultaneous shifts of carbon emissions from the United Kingdom to other countries in the EU ETS. The additional emission cuts in the United Kingdom may thus have rather increased the intake of emission permits into the Market Stability Reserve (MSR) of the EU ETS than increased emissions outside the United Kingdom. For a detailed analysis of how policies accompanying the EU ETS affect emissions over time see Perino et al. (2019[30]).

[3] This recent example from the EU ETS illustrates the effectiveness of carbon pricing by considering the carbon price elasticity, i.e. how much do emissions change, when the carbon price increases. The mechanisms that underlie the observation of an increase in carbon prices and a corresponding decline in emissions are complex. Annex A makes a short attempt to reveal some important mechanisms behind the increase of permit prices and reduction of emissions.

3 How far do we need to go (to decarbonise)?

This chapter asks the question how high carbon prices need to be to reach the goal of net-zero carbon emissions by mid-century. It reviews studies on the topic and proposes three benchmarks. First, EUR 30 per tonne of CO_2 as an historic low-end benchmark of carbon costs. Second, EUR 60 per tonne of CO_2 as mid-range estimate for carbon costs in 2020, and at the same time low-end estimate for carbon costs in 2030. Third, EUR 120 per tonne of CO_2 as a central estimate for carbon costs in 2030.

Aiming to limit global temperature increases to 1.5°C, as called for in the Paris Agreement, requires decarbonisation by about mid-century (Rogelj et al., 2018[14]; Rogelj et al., 2015[15]).[1] Kaufman et al. (2020[16]) estimate that decarbonising by 2060 requires a carbon price of about EUR 30 per tonne CO_2 in 2025 for the example of the United States.[2] In 2030, the same decarbonisation goal requires a carbon price that is twice as large: EUR 60 per tonne CO_2. Decarbonising by 2050, which is more in line with the 1.5°C goal, by their estimates requires a carbon price of EUR 100 in 2030. If, in addition, carbon pricing is supposed to play a role as a major decarbonisation tool (which would almost certainly increase economic efficiency and lower aggregate emission abatement costs), carbon prices would need to be higher by EUR 20, equalling about EUR 120 per tonne of CO_2 in total (see Figure 2, "low complementary" policies in Kaufman et al. (2020[16]))[3].

Earlier estimates, by the High-Level Commission on Carbon Prices (2017[17]), show that carbon prices at a level of EUR 40-80 per tonne CO_2 are needed in 2020 for countries to decarbonise in line with the Paris Agreement. In 2030, prices should reach EUR 50-100 per tonne of CO_2. The IMF recommends an increase in carbon prices by EUR 75 per tonne of CO_2 from current levels through 2030 in a scenario that assumes optimal support for clean technology development (IMF, 2019[18]). Based on a less technologically optimistic scenario, the Quinet Commission (2019[19]) recommends a carbon price of EUR 52 per tonne of CO_2 in 2018, increasing to EUR 250 in 2030 and EUR 775 in 2050,[4] which is levied in addition to the baseline of fuel taxes in France in 2017.[5]

A different approach is to estimate the damage that results from one tonne of CO_2 released into the atmosphere. Under this approach, it is economical to cut emissions, as long the investment needed to reduce emissions is lower than the costs of emissions to society.[6] Estimates vary considerably due to different assumptions, for example, how future consumption is valued compared to current consumption, and what types of damage are taken into account. The German Environmental Protection Agency estimates the social damage to be EUR 180 per tonne of CO_2 released in 2016. An earlier literature review by Alberici et al. (2014[20]) suggested a low-end estimate of climate cost of EUR 30 at that time.

Against this background, this edition of Effective Carbon Rates employs three carbon price benchmarks:

- EUR 30 per tonne of CO_2, a historic low-end price benchmark of carbon costs in the early and mid-2010s (Alberici et al., 2014[20]). A carbon price of EUR 30 in 2025 is also still consistent with the slow decarbonisation scenario by 2060 according to Kaufman et al. (2020[16]).

- EUR 60 per tonne of CO_2, low-end 2030 and mid-range 2020 benchmark according to the High-Level Commission on Carbon Pricing (2017[17]). A carbon price of EUR 60 in 2030 is also consistent with the slow decarbonisation scenario by 2060 according to Kaufman et al. (2020[16]).

- EUR 120 per tonne CO_2, a central estimate of the carbon price needed in 2030 to decarbonise by mid-century under the assumption that carbon pricing plays a major role in the overall decarbonisation effort (See Figure 2 , low complementary policies in Kaufman et al. (2020[16])). EUR 120 is also more in line with recent estimates of overall social carbon costs.

EUR 30 and EUR 60 per tonne of CO_2 have already been applied in earlier editions of Effective Carbon Rates and thus allow for comparison over time. EUR 120 is a new benchmark that allows assessing progress towards carbon prices in the near future that are in line with current decarbonisation goals.

References

Alberici, S. et al. (2014), *Subsidies and Costs of EU Energy – Final Report and Annex 3*, Ecofys.   [7]

High-Level Commission on Carbon Prices (2017), *Report of the High-Level Commission on Carbon Prices*, World Bank, Washington, D.C., https://static1.squarespace.com/static/54ff9c5ce4b0a53decccfb4c/t/59b7f2409f8dce5316811 916/1505227332748/CarbonPricing_FullReport.pdf (accessed on 16 February 2018). [4]

IMF (2019), *Fiscal Monitor: How to Mitigate Climate Change*, IMF, Washington, D.C. [5]

Kaufman, N. et al. (2020), "A near-term to net zero alternative to the social cost of carbon for setting carbon prices", *Nature Climate Change*, http://dx.doi.org/10.1038/s41558-020-0880-3. [3]

Quinet, A. (2019), *La valeur de l'action pour le climat. Une valeur tutélaire du carbone pour évaluer les investissements et les politiques publiques*, France Stratégie, Paris, https://www.strategie.gouv.fr/sites/strategie.gouv.fr/files/atoms/files/fs-2019-rapport-la-valeur-de-laction-pour-le-climat_0.pdf (accessed on 24 July 2019). [6]

Rogelj, J. et al. (2015), "Energy system transformations for limiting end-of-century warming to below 1.5 °C", *Nature Climate Change*, Vol. 5, pp. 519-527, http://dx.doi.org/10.1038/nclimate2572. [2]

Rogelj, J. et al. (2018), "Mitigation Pathways Compatible with 1.5°C in the Context of Sustainable Development", in Masson-Delmotte, V. et al. (eds.), *Global Warming of 1.5°C. An IPCC Special Report on the impacts of global warming of 1.5°C.*, IPCC. [1]

Notes

[1] In the Paris Agreement signatories agreed to aim for limiting global average temperature increases to 1.5°C compared to pre-industrial levels and ensuring that global average temperature increases remain well below 2°C. Many model simulations predict that the 1.5°C goal requires net-zero emissions in the 2050s, while for a 2°C goal net-zero emissions by 2070 can be sufficient (Rogelj et al., 2018[14]). In addition, the amount of emissions that could potentially be removed from the atmosphere affects the pathway to net-zero emissions.

[2] This document assumes long-term EUR-USD parity.

[3] Carbon pricing is generally not the lead decarbonisation instrument in the jurisdictions where it exists. Some emissions trading systems instead work as a backstop rather than as the prime decarbonisation tool. This is the case when there are many other policies such as efficiency standards, technology phase outs, clean energy requirements etc. that are more stringent than the carbon price that results from the emission cap. In this case, the cap works as a backstop to ensure that aggregate emission targets are reached. In such a case permit prices can be expected to be low or remain close to the minimum carbon price of the system, if such a minimum price exists. For example, permit prices in the California Cap-and-Trade-Program have so far been very close to the corresponding reserve prices for permit auctions.

[4] Keeping the decarbonisation objective by mid-century in mind, there will be few emissions for which the very high carbon price needs to be paid.

[5] The Quinet Commission baseline scenario corresponds to the French effective carbon rates in 2017, excluding the French carbon tax and the EU ETS permit price.

[6] Emissions can also be reduced through behavioural change in some cases, not requiring a monetary investment.

4 Attainment of near term carbon pricing benchmarks, the carbon pricing score and the gap

This chapter highlights key results on the state of carbon pricing in 44 OECD and G20 countries. It introduces the carbon pricing score as summary indicator for carbon pricing efforts. Results are provided for the 44 countries as a group, as well as by country and by sector in 2018. A divergence in progress made since 2015 is observed between the countries that are most advanced with carbon pricing and those that are least advanced. The rear part of the chapter provides an outlook on the impacts of recent developments in emissions trading in China and the European Union on carbon pricing scores.

The *Carbon Pricing Score (CPS)* measures the extent to which countries have attained the goal of pricing all energy related carbon emissions at certain benchmark values for carbon costs or more. The more progress that a country has made towards the relevant benchmark value, the higher the CPS. For example, a CPS of 100% against a EUR 30 per tonne CO_2 benchmark means that the country (or the group of countries) prices all carbon emissions in its (their) territory from energy use at EUR 30 or more. A CPS of 0% means that the country prices no emissions at all. An intermediate CPS between 0% and 100% means that some emissions are priced, but that not all emissions are priced at a level that equals or exceeds the benchmark. Similarly, a EUR 60 or EUR 120 CPS of 100% means that all emissions are priced at a level that equals or exceeds EUR 60 or EUR 120 per tonne CO_2.

The *Effective Carbon Rates* database reports the CPS for the following three benchmarks: First, EUR 30 per tonne of CO_2, which is an historic low-end price benchmark of carbon costs (CPS_{30}). Second, EUR 60 per tonne of CO_2, which is a forward looking 2030 low-end and mid-range 2020 benchmark (CPS_{60}). Third, EUR 120 per tonne of CO_2, which is a central estimate of the carbon costs in 2030 (CPS_{120}). For the presentation of key results, this document focuses on the CPS_{60}. The *Effective Carbon Rates* database on OECD.STAT will show results for all three carbon pricing scores (CPS_{30}, CPS_{60} and CPS_{120}).

Earlier versions of *Effective Carbon Rates* summarised the state of carbon pricing using the carbon pricing gap. The gap measures the extent to which carbon prices fall short of various benchmarks for carbon costs. Readers can calculate the carbon pricing gap at a certain benchmark (BM) value by subtracting the CPS from 100%, i.e. $Carbon\ Pricing\ Gap_{BM} = 100\% - Carbon\ Pricing\ Score_{BM}$. Figure 4.1 below illustrates this relationship.

In 2018, the 44 OECD and G20 countries analysed, which are responsible for about 80% of energy related global CO_2 emissions, had a CPS_{60} of 19%, i.e. they reached 19% of the goal of pricing all emissions at EUR 60 or more per tonne of CO_2; see the area shaded in light blue in Figure 4.1. The corresponding *carbon pricing gap* was 81% (i.e. 100% - 19%) and is shown in dark blue.

Figure 4.1. The Carbon Pricing Score

The group of 44 OECD and G20 countries together reached 19% of the benchmark of pricing all emissions at EUR 60 or more per tonne CO_2 in 2018

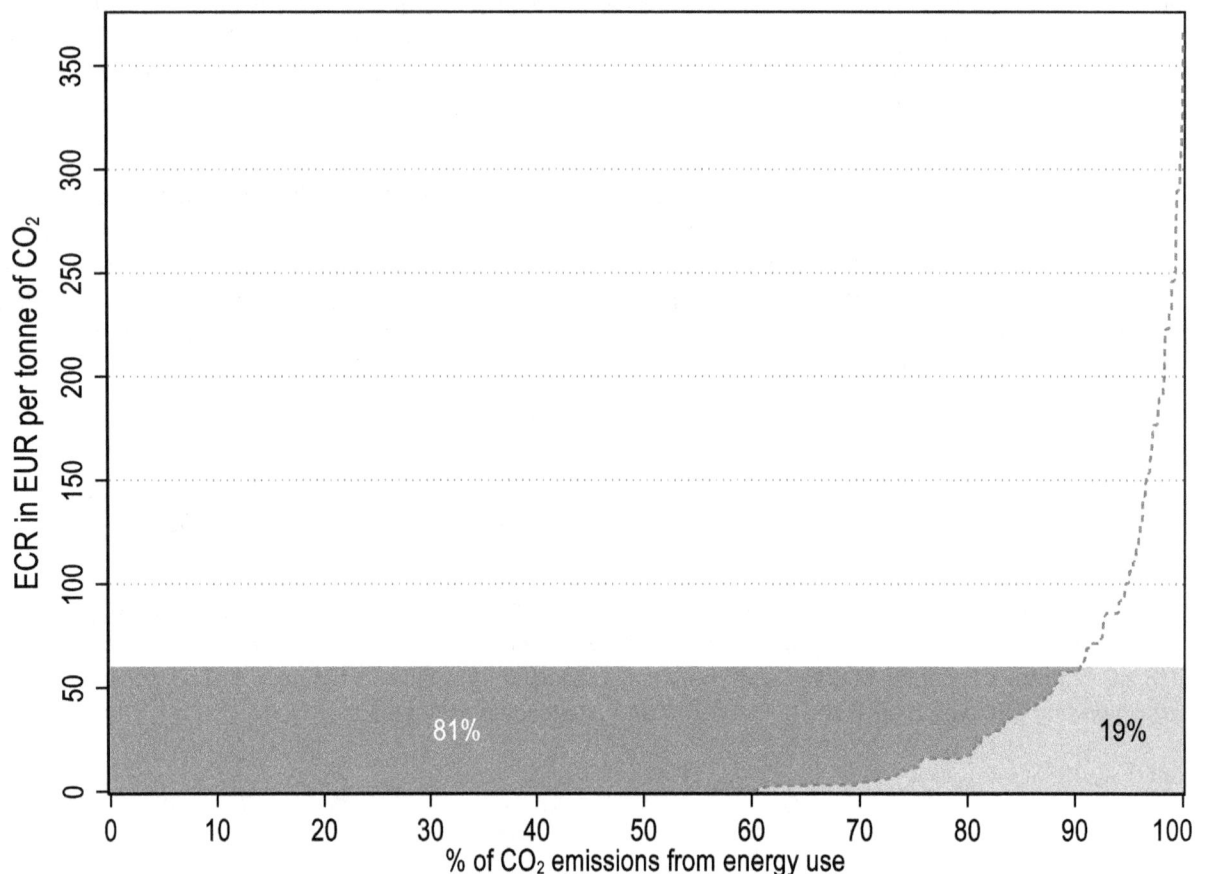

Note: The area shaded in light blue shows the *Carbon Pricing Score* (CPS) at EUR 60 per tonne CO_2 (CPS60). It shows the extent to which the group of 44 OECD and G20 countries together reached the benchmark to price all emissions from energy use at least at EUR 60 per tonne CO_2 in 2018. The area shaded in dark blue shows the *Carbon Pricing Gap*, i.e. the shortfall to pricing all emissions at least at EUR 60 per tonne CO_2.

Stronger progress had been made towards the more moderate EUR 30 benchmark, but the CPS30 is still just under a quarter (24%). Considering the more ambitious and forward-looking central carbon pricing benchmark of EUR 120 in 2030, the CPS120 was only 12% in the 44 countries in 2018.

The light and dark blue area in Figure 4.1 together provide a revenue estimate of a uniform carbon price of EUR 60 per tonne CO_2, showing that there is still significant revenue potential from strengthening carbon pricing. See Marten and Van Dender (2019[21]) for estimates of potential revenue from carbon pricing, and a survey of how countries make use of the revenue from carbon pricing.

Across the 44 countries, there was hardly any progress with carbon pricing between 2018 and 2015. However, between 2012 and 2015 the CPS60 improved by 3 percentage points.

Fuel excise taxes dominate effective marginal and effective average carbon rates

Looking at the components of carbon prices, 93% of the overall price signal resulted from taxes; 89 percentage points of the 93% were the result of fuel taxes, while the other 4 percentage points resulted from carbon taxes. Countries generally implement both fuel and carbon taxes through fuel excise taxation, but a distinction is made here based on whether a jurisdiction labels a certain tax to be a carbon tax or not. The remaining 7% of the price signal results from permit prices.

To account for the commonly observed free-allocation of some or all emission permits, this edition of *Effective Carbon Rates* calculates effective *average* carbon rates (EACRs) in addition to the already existing effective *marginal* carbon rates (EMCRs).[1] The EACR adjusts the effective carbon rate for any free allocation of tradeable emission permits. Thereby, the EACR captures the effect of free allocation on total expected profits and the ranking of zero- and low-carbon versus high-carbon investment projects, and thus allows for a comparison of the incentives to invest in zero- and low-carbon technologies (Flues and van Dender, 2017[22]; Flues and van Dender, 2020[23]).

Box 4.1. Effective marginal carbon rates (EMCRs) and effective average carbon rates (EACRs)

Carbon prices vary in how their rate applies to the entire carbon emission base. Fuel and carbon taxes generally apply at one (or several) rates without exemptions or reductions for a certain fuel or carbon emission base. Energy users thus pay the rate that applies for their energy use for all emissions. If fuel or carbon taxes include tax-free allowances, this implies that emitters do not have to pay the tax for all emissions. For example, tax-free allowances in the South African carbon tax imply that emitters have to pay only for 5% of their emissions (Roelf, 2019[24]). Tax-free allowances drive a wedge between the marginal price emitters pay for an additional unit of emissions and the average price they pay for their entire emissions.

Emission trading systems generally allocate permits via permit auctions and some form of free permit allocation. Any free allocation of permits in an ETS reduces the effective carbon emission base, for which the emitter needs to buy permits. Free allocation of permits also drives a wedge between marginal and average carbon prices, much like tax allowances do for taxes. Considering the same set of emissions, emissions trading and effective carbon taxation are equivalent in terms of their effective emission base coverage when permits are fully auctioned and no tax-free allowances are granted.

Taxes with uniform carbon rates for all emissions and emission trading systems with full permit auctioning provide stronger incentives for investment in clean technologies than taxes with tax-free allowances and emission trading systems with benchmarking or allocation based on historical emissions (Flues and van Dender, 2017[22]). Tax-free allowances, benchmarking and allocation based on historical emissions affect economic rents, and the current allocation rules tend to do so in ways that favour carbon-intensive technologies.

The effective average carbon rate (EACR) adjusts for any tax-free allowances and free permit allocation. It captures the effect of allowances and permit allocations on total expected profits and thus on project rankings. In other words, the strength of the incentives to invest in clean technologies can be compared across different tax and emission trading systems by comparing their EACRs. The effective marginal carbon rate (EMCR) shows the strength of the marginal incentive to reduce emissions, e.g. via small-scale efficiency improvements or demand reductions for an investment that has already been carried out.

Sources: Flues and Van Dender (2017[22]; 2020[23])

The effective average CPS$_{60}$ for the group of 44 countries together was 17% in 2018, i.e. countries reached 17% of the goal of pricing all carbon emissions from energy use with an EACR of at least EUR 60 per tonne of CO_2. The score is about 1.5 percentage point lower than for the (effective marginal) carbon pricing score. This limited deviation reflects that, even though free permit allocation is common in emissions trading systems, permit prices only account for 7% of the total marginal carbon-pricing signal. The contribution of effective average permit prices to the total effective average carbon price signal is correspondingly lower than in the case of marginal rates, namely 3%. The effective average CPS_{30} was 22% in 2018, and the effective average CPS_{120} was 12%.

Divergence in carbon pricing progress

Figure 4.2 shows countries' CPS_{60} in 2018 on the horizontal axis, and the change in their CPS_{60} between 2015 and 2018 on the vertical axis. Countries with a higher CPS_{60} increased their CPS_{60} between 2015 and 2018 on average more than countries with a lower CPS_{60}.[2]

Figure 4.2. Between 2015 and 2018, carbon pricing scores increased most where they were relatively high

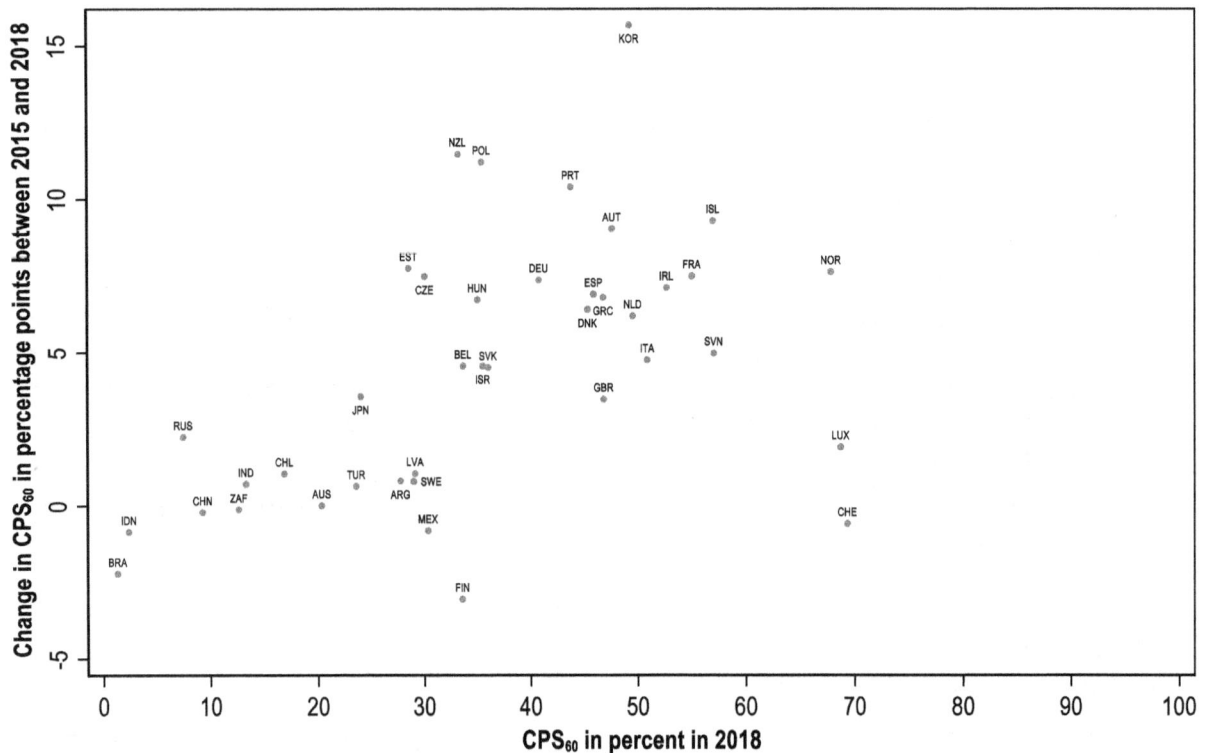

The ten countries with the highest CPS_{60} in 2018 achieved more than half (52%) of the goal of pricing all emissions at EUR 60 or more per tonne of CO_2 in 2018.[3] These countries reached a CPS_{30} of 71% and a CPS_{120} of 39%.

Significant progress is observed for these ten leading countries between 2015 and 2018; they advanced by around 6 percentage points towards the low-end 2030 benchmark of pricing all emissions at EUR 60 or more per tonne of CO_2, or 1.8 percentage points per year. If the ten leading countries continue to make similar progress on carbon pricing, their CPS_{60} would rise to 74% by 2030. For pricing all emissions at EUR 60 per tonne CO_2 or more by 2030, they would need to increase the CPS_{60} by 4 percentage points per year.

Many of these ten countries participate in the EU ETS. The recent reform of the EU ETS with the introduction of the Market Stability Reserve (MSR) helped to increase permit prices in the EU ETS from about EUR 5 in 2017 to about EUR 25 today. The higher permit prices are a major factor explaining the progress in carbon pricing by these countries. Other factors relate to stronger carbon prices in some countries for the residential and commercial sector. Korea´s strong progress with carbon pricing is largely due to an increase in the permit prices of its broad-based emissions trading system.

By contrast, the ten countries with the lowest CPS_{60} in 2018 together reached a CPS_{60} of 13% in 2018. The CPS_{30} was 16% and the CPS_{120} was 7% in 2018. These countries made no progress between 2015 and 2018 on the CPS_{60}.

The strength of carbon pricing varies across sectors

In the road sector, in 2018 the CPS_{60} was 80%, the CPS_{30} was 91%, while the CPS_{120} stood at 58%. The other external costs of road usage (such as accidents, noise, local air pollution and congestion), however, exceed climate costs by far. Thus, there are good reasons for charging effective carbon rates that are substantially higher than low-end and mid-point estimates of climate costs in the road sector.[4] For a more detailed discussion of the social costs of road usage and economic instruments that advance user contributions, see Van Dender (2019[25]).

Table 4.1. Progress varies significantly across sectors

Effective Marginal Carbon Pricing Scores by sector for the group of 44 OECD and G20 countries together

Effective Marginal Carbon Pricing Score			
Sector	EUR 30	EUR 60	EUR 120
Agriculture & Fisheries	43%	38%	23%
Electricity	10%	5%	3%
Industry	9%	5%	3%
Off-road Transport	34%	25%	13%
Residential & Commercial	14%	10%	6%
Road Transport	91%	80%	58%

In the electricity sector, CPS_{60} was 5%, the CPS_{30} was 10% and the CPS_{120} was 3% in 2018. However, some countries achieved significantly higher carbon pricing scores in the electricity sector. Both Korea and Iceland reached a CPS_{30} of 93%, and the United Kingdom scored 77% in 2018. All three countries also attained a CPS_{60} of 50%. In the United Kingdom, emitters need to pay for all emission permits from the EU ETS and need to pay a tax (the carbon price support) in addition to the permits. This results in a significant effective carbon rate for fossil fuels of about EUR 36 per tonne of CO_2 in 2018. Since 2012, the year before the carbon price support was introduced, carbon emissions in the UK electricity sector fell by 73%. Korea, where emitters still receive almost all emission permits for free, did not show a strong decline in emissions from the electricity sector.[5]

In the industry sector, in 2018 all countries combined scored a CPS_{60} of 5%, a CPS_{30} of 9%, and a CPS_{120} of 3 %. Norway, Slovenia and Korea reached a CPS_{60} of 33% and a CPS_{30} of 50% or more. Considering the effective average carbon pricing score, all countries combined scored a CPS_{60} of 3%. This results from a significant share of permit prices in the overall carbon-pricing signal (nearly 50%) and a large share of free allocation for industrial facilities that are subject to carbon pricing.

In the residential and commercial sector, the CPS_{60} was 10% for all 44 countries together in 2018. The CPS_{30} was 14% and the CPS_{120} 6%. Some countries achieved a significantly higher carbon pricing level in the residential and commercial sector. The Netherlands reached a CPS_{60} of 90%, while Switzerland achieved a CPS_{60} of 78% and Italy, France and Greece achieved a CPS_{60} of about 50%. Five countries achieved a CPS_{30} of more than 70% (Netherlands, Iceland, Switzerland, Korea and Ireland). With the exception of Korea, which prices emissions in the residential and commercial sector through emissions trading, effective carbon rates in the residential and commercial sector result mainly from the use of taxes on fossil fuels, sometimes also labelled explicitly as carbon taxes.

A handful of carbon pricing leaders attain high carbon pricing scores

In 2018, Switzerland, Luxembourg and Norway reached a CPS60 of close to 70%. In Switzerland, the high CPS60 is the result of fuel taxes in the road sector that are fully earmarked for road infrastructure purposes, a significant carbon incentive tax (CHF 96 or EUR 83 per tonne CO2 since 2018) for fossil fuel use in the residential and commercial sector, a highly decarbonised electricity supply and few industrial emissions, that are largely subject to the Swiss ETS. In Norway, this is the result of a highly decarbonised electricity supply, significant taxes on fossil fuels used in the residential and commercial sector, as well as a large share of industrial sector emissions resulting from the offshore petroleum industry, that is subject to both a carbon tax and the EU ETS. In Luxembourg, a small country with a significant share of daily commuters who live abroad, a high share of transit traffic and considerable fuel tourism, the high CPS_{60} is largely due to the road sector dominating overall energy use. Even though road fuel taxes in Luxembourg are lower than in its neighbouring countries, the fact that road fuels have generally a higher effective carbon rate than other sectors (see also the previous section) leads to the high carbon pricing score for Luxembourg. While given the specific circumstances it is challenging to translate the carbon pricing score for Luxembourg in a certain carbon pricing effort, it is worth noting that Luxembourg levies a carbon tax from 2021 onwards.

Table 4.2. Some countries attain high carbon pricing scores

Carbon pricing score at EUR 60 per tonne CO_2	
CHE	69%
LUX	69%
NOR	68%
SVN	57%
ISL	57%
FRA	55%
IRL	53%
ITA	51%
NLD	50%
KOR	49%
AUT	48%
GBR	47%
GRC	47%
ESP	46%
DNK	45%
LTU	45%
PRT	44%
DEU	41%
SVK	36%
ISR	36%
POL	35%
HUN	35%
CAN	34%
BEL	34%
FIN	34%
NZL	33%

MEX	30%
CZE	30%
LVA	29%
SWE	29%
EST	29%
ARG	28%
COL	25%
JPN	24%
TUR	24%
USA	22%
AUS	20%
CHL	17%
IND	13%
ZAF	13%
CHN	9%
RUS	7%
IDN	2%
BRA	1%

Note: This table includes emission from the combustion of biomass in the emission base. Results excluding emissions from the combustion of biomass are available in Annex 4.A as well as on OECD.STAT.

Nearly a quarter of the analysed countries (10 out of 44) had a CPS_{60} of around 50% or more in 2018, i.e. they had achieved the goal of pricing all carbon emissions at least at the midpoint benchmark for carbon costs in 2020 and the low-end benchmark for carbon costs in 2030 by more than a half. These countries have in common that they price emissions from the road sector significantly, have moderate to high carbon prices for fossil fuel use in the residential and commercial sector and many participate in or are linked to the EU ETS, which prices emissions from the electricity generation and industry. Korea, with a CPS_{60} of 49% in 2018, has a broad based emission trading system, which contributes 30% to its overall carbon pricing effort, while the remaining 70% results from taxes on fuel use.

The previous section showed that carbon pricing scores differ across sectors when considering all 44 together (see Table 4.1). In addition, the section mentioned substantial variation in carbon pricing scores within sectors across countries. While a full discussion of results by country, by sector is beyond the scope of this report, the Effective Carbon Rates database on OECD.STAT provides carbon pricing scores by country for six economic sectors.

Reforms can increase the carbon pricing score

While China had a CPS_{60} of only 9% in 2018, the introduction of a national ETS in February 2021 increased its CPS significantly. In a first step, China included the electricity sector in its national ETS. Assuming that the national ETS covers 3.6 billion tonnes of carbon emissions from the electricity sector in the first step (Zhang, 2020[26]) at an estimated carbon price of 43 CNY (EUR 5.51) per tonne CO_2 (Slater et al., 2019[27]), this increased its CPS_{60} to 12% and its CPS_{30} to 16%.[6] In a second step, China plans to also include emissions from industrial facilities into its national ETS. Based on estimates for this development phase, (Zhang, 2020[26]) the system will cover all Chinese electricity sector emissions and about 60% of all industrial emissions. Together with an expected permit price of CNY 75 (EUR 9.60) per tonne CO_2 in 2025 (Slater et al., 2019[27]), the CPS_{60} would then increase to 19% and the CPS_{30} to 29%. As a result, the overall CPS_{60} for all countries together would increase to 22%, and the CPS_{30} to 31%, reflecting the significant share of Chinese emissions in the total emissions of the 44 OECD and G20 countries considered in this report.

Table 4.3. ETS reform can increase the carbon pricing score

Estimated effect of the Chinese National ETS and higher permit prices in the EU ETS on the carbon pricing score

Country or group	Scenario	CPS30	CPS60
China	Status quo in 2018	10%	9%
China	National ETS covers 3.3. billion tonnes CO_2 from electricity generation at an estimated carbon price of CNY 43 (EUR 5.51) per tonne CO_2	16%	12%
China	National ETS covers 100 % of electricity sector emissions plus 60% of industrial emissions at an estimated carbon price of CNY 75 (EUR 9.60) per tonne CO_2	29%	19%
EU 23	Status quo 2018	57%	44%
EU 23	Permit prices increase to EUR 30 per tonne CO_2	73%	52%
EU 23	ETS expands to cover also residential and commercial emissions as well as emissions from small industrial facilities. Permit prices increase to EUR 30 (& EUR 60) per tonne CO_2 respectively	85%	61% (84%)

Note: The estimates do not consider any demand response to the ETS reforms. See this chapter's endnote 6 for additional detail.

Prices in the EU ETS have increased since 2018 and trade above EUR 30 per tonne of CO_2 since early January 2021. With the announcement of the Green Deal and the goal to achieve climate neutrality by 2050 a further increase of permit prices is possible. At permit prices in the EU ETS of EUR 30 or above, the CPS_{30} for the 23 EU countries considered in this document increases from 57% in 2018 to 73%. In addition, the CPS_{60} increases from 44% in 2018 to 52% with a permit price of EUR 30 per tonne of CO_2. To close the carbon pricing gap entirely - pricing all emissions at EUR 30 (or EUR 60) or more per tonne of CO_2 - carbon prices would also need to increase in the sectors that are currently not covered by the EU ETS and that have low effective carbon rates. In particular, many countries charge only very moderate effective carbon rates in the residential and commercial sector, while some levy significant carbon prices through fuel excise taxes (e.g. the Netherlands) or explicit carbon taxes (e.g. Switzerland, which is linked to the EU ETS).

If the EU ETS were expanded to include all fossil fuel emissions from the residential and commercial sector as well as from industry, the CPS_{30} would increase to 85%, assuming a permit price of EUR 30 per tonne CO_2. The remaining gap to pricing all emissions at EUR 30 or more would result largely from biofuels, which often have an effective carbon rate of zero, or a substantially lower rate than those of comparable fossil fuels. The CPS_{60} would increase to 61%. If in addition permit prices increased to at least EUR 60 per tonne CO_2, the CPS_{60} would increase to 84%.

Annex 4.A. The carbon pricing score excluding emissions from the combustion of biomass

This Annex provides results for the carbon pricing score across countries excluding emissions from the combustion of biomass. Additional results excluding emissions from biomass are available on OECD.STAT.

The results excluding emissions from the combustion of biomass complement the results including emissions from biomass. The latter are shown by default in line with previous editions of Taxing Energy Use (OECD, 2013[3]; OECD, 2015[4]; OECD, 2018[5]; OECD, 2019[1]), as well as Effective Carbon Rates (OECD, 2016[2]; OECD, 2018[6]) as well as considering recent evidence on lifecycle emissions from biofuels. Nevertheless, the *biomass exclusion* approach may be of interest to specific countries and users as it may better reflect local conditions or improve comparability with other inventories.

Annex 3.A of Effective Carbon Rates 2018 (OECD, 2018[6]) discusses the implications of including and of excluding emissions from the combustion of biomass in more detail.

Annex Table 4.A.1. Carbon pricing score at EUR 60 per tonne CO_2

Excluding emissions from the combustion of biomass

	Carbon Pricing Score at EUR 60 per tonne CO_2 (CPS_{60})
CHE	84%
NOR	77%
LUX	71%
LTU	70%
DNK	69%
SVN	67%
FRA	63%
AUT	63%
FIN	63%
SWE	62%
ISL	61%
ITA	58%
LVA	57%
PRT	56%
IRL	55%
NLD	52%
GBR	52%
KOR	50%
ESP	50%
GRC	49%
DEU	45%
HUN	42%
SVK	40%
NZL	39%
POL	38%
BEL	37%

CAN	37%
ISR	36%
EST	36%
CZE	34%
MEX	33%
COL	32%
ARG	30%
JPN	25%
CHL	25%
TUR	24%
USA	22%
AUS	21%
IND	18%
ZAF	14%
CHN	10%
RUS	8%
IDN	3%
BRA	2%

References

Flues, F. and K. van Dender (2020), "Carbon pricing design: Effectiveness, efficiency and feasibility: An investment perspective", *OECD Taxation Working Papers*, No. 48, OECD Publishing, Paris, https://dx.doi.org/10.1787/91ad6a1e-en. [3]

Flues, F. and K. van Dender (2017), "Permit allocation rules and investment incentives in emissions trading systems", *OECD Taxation Working Papers*, No. 33, OECD Publishing, Paris, https://dx.doi.org/10.1787/c3acf05e-en. [2]

Marten, M. and K. van Dender (2019), "The use of revenues from carbon pricing", *OECD Taxation Working Papers*, No. 43, OECD Publishing, Paris, https://dx.doi.org/10.1787/3cb265e4-en. [1]

OECD (2019), *Taxing Energy Use 2019: Using Taxes for Climate Action*, OECD Publishing, Paris, https://dx.doi.org/10.1787/058ca239-en. [11]

OECD (2018), *Effective Carbon Rates 2018. Pricing Carbon Emissions Through Taxes and Emissions Trading*, OECD Publishing, Paris, https://doi.org/10.1787/9789264305304-en. [13]

OECD (2018), *Taxing Energy Use 2018: Companion to the Taxing Energy Use Database*, OECD Publishing, Paris. [10]

OECD (2016), *Effective Carbon Rates: Pricing CO2 through Taxes and Emissions Trading Systems*, OECD Publishing, Paris, https://dx.doi.org/10.1787/9789264260115-en. [12]

OECD (2015), *Taxing Energy Use 2015: OECD and Selected Partner Economies*, OECD Publishing, Paris, https://dx.doi.org/10.1787/9789264232334-en. [9]

OECD (2013), *Taxing Energy Use: A Graphical Analysis*, OECD Publishing, Paris, https://dx.doi.org/10.1787/9789264183933-en. [8]

Roelf, W. (2019), "South African parliament approves long-delayed carbon tax bill - Reuters", *Reuters*, https://www.reuters.com/article/us-safrica-carbontax/south-african-parliament-approves-long-delayed-carbon-tax-bill-idUSKCN1Q81U8 (accessed on 7 May 2019).   [4]

Slater, H. et al. (2019), *2019 China Carbon Pricing Survey*, China Carbon Forum.   [7]

Van Dender, K. (2019), "Taxing vehicles, fuels, and road use: opportunities for improving transport tax practice", *OECD Taxation Working Papers*, No. 44, OECD Publishing, Paris, https://doi.org/10.1787/fd193abd-en.   [5]

Zhang, X. (2020), *Estimates for emission coverage of Chinese emissions trading systems*.   [6]

Notes

[1] This document reports effective marginal carbon rates by default. If effective average carbon rates are shown the term "effective average" is always explicitly mentioned.

[2] Higher effective carbon rates are expected to reduce emissions over time. If all emissions of a jurisdiction are priced at the benchmark value (for carbon costs) or more, the corresponding CPS will remain at 100%. If, however, many rates are below the benchmark and rates are increased for some emissions only, it can happen that subsequently only those emissions decline for which the price increase applies. As a result, the share of the higher priced emissions in overall emissions declines over time. The effect on the CPS would be an initial increase in the CPS (immediately after the rate increase and before the emission decline), that, overtime, is counteracted by a decreasing share of higher priced emissions.

[3] Table 4.2 lists countries by the CPS_{60}.

[4] Considering air pollution more generally, there also good reasons to charge higher carbon prices than what low-and mid-point estimates of carbon costs suggest in other non-transport sectors. For example, air pollution from coal, oil, gas and wood combustion for electricity generation and heating purposes in the industry sector and the residential and commercial sector, provide an economic argument for effective carbon rates that exceed low- and mid-point estimates of carbon costs.

[5] The effective average carbon pricing score at EUR 30 and EUR 60 per tonne of CO_2 were 42% and 21% respectively in 2018, reflecting a significant share of free allocation in the Korean electricity sectors, which mutes the incentives to invest in cleaner power generation and reduce emissions.

[6] The estimates of ETS reforms described in this section do not include any demand response. To evaluate the effects of higher effective carbon rates on emissions and the CPS, consider that if a jurisdiction increases its CPS, the higher effective carbon rates are expected to reduce emissions where they apply. If the jurisdiction increases its CPS to 100%, emissions are expected to decline, but this will not change the CPS. However, if a jurisdiction only increases its CPS in one sector to 100%, emissions in this sector are expected to decrease, but in the absence of other policies not in the other sectors. After an initial increase in the jurisdiction-wide CPS, due to the carbon pricing increase in one sector, the jurisdiction-wide CPS may thus decrease over time to the extent that sectors with lower effective carbon rates gain more weight in the share of jurisdiction-wide emissions.

5 The bigger carbon pricing picture

This chapter considers the relationship between carbon pricing, carbon efficiency and economic output across economies. Countries with higher carbon pricing scores tend to be more carbon efficient, as measured by carbon emissions per unit of economic output. Likewise, countries that increase their carbon pricing scores also become more carbon efficient. In addition, countries more advanced with carbon pricing also tend to produce more economic output per capita, and countries that progress more with carbon pricing show a stronger increase in economic output per capita.

This chapter considers the relationship between the CPS, and the emission intensity of GDP (a climate perspective) and GDP per capita (an economic output perspective).

Climate effects

Figure 5.1 shows that countries that have a higher CPS are, on average, also more carbon efficient, i.e. they emit fewer emissions per unit of GDP. Figure 5.2 shows the same relationship but considering *changes* in the CPS and relating them to *changes* in the carbon emission intensity of GDP. Countries that increase their CPS are shown on the right side of Figure 5.2, i.e. their change in the score is positive. On average, these countries have also experienced a decrease in their carbon intensity of GDP, which shows from a negative change in the carbon intensity of GDP, meaning that they are located in the bottom half of the graph.

Figure 5.1 does not necessarily imply a direct causal effect in either direction. Low emissions per unit of GDP can be the result of a high carbon pricing score steering the economy towards zero- and low-emission energy sources. Alternatively, countries with fewer emissions per unit of GDP may find it easier to price emissions. Figure 5.2 controls for unobserved country-specific effects that are constant over time, ruling out that a low-carbon intensity of GDP is entirely explained by factors other a high CPS. Nevertheless, it could be the case that countries that decrease their carbon intensity of GDP simultaneously increase their CPS, e.g. if carbon pricing is enacted together with a suite of other climate polices. In such circumstances, it is difficult to estimate the exact contribution of a higher CPS on carbon efficiency.

Notwithstanding the caveats in interpreting Figure 5.1 and Figure 5.2 there is strong empirical evidence that clearly shows that higher carbon prices lower emissions, see for example the literature reviews by Arlinghaus (2015[7]) and Martin et al. (2016[8]). Carefully identifying the effects of higher effective carbon rates, Sen and Vollebergh (2018[9]) find that a EUR 10 per tonne of CO_2 increase in the effective carbon rates is expected to lead to a 7.3% reduction in carbon emissions on average.

Figure 5.1. Countries with a higher carbon pricing score are more carbon efficient

Carbon intensity of GDP and carbon pricing score in 2018

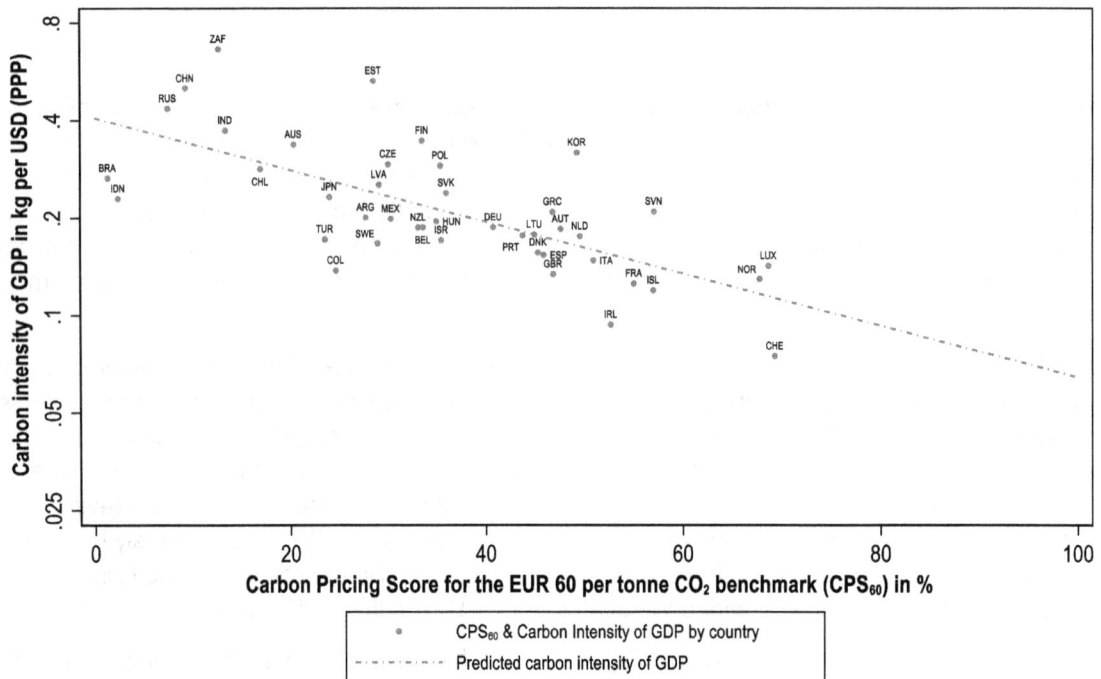

Reading Note: The graph shows that countries that have a higher carbon pricing score towards the benchmark of EUR 60 per tonne CO_2 (a low-end benchmark for carbon costs in 2030) have a lower carbon intensity of GDP.
Source: GDP data from the World Development Indicators (World Bank, 2020[28])

The association of a higher CPS with a lower emission intensity of GDP is consistent with the notion that by pricing all emissions at a minimum of EUR 60 per tonne of CO_2, countries can make significant progress towards the net-zero emissions goal, but that carbon-neutrality by mid-century very likely requires additional efforts. To illustrate, a simple log-linear regression of the CPS_{60} on the carbon intensity of GDP (Figure 5.1) reveals that a one percentage point increase in the CPS_{60} is associated with a 1.8 percent decrease in the carbon intensity of GDP. By this log-linear relationship, countries that reach a CPS_{60} of 100, would be expected to lower their carbon emission intensity to around 0.06 kg per unit of GDP over time. Scenarios by Peters et al. (2017, p. 120[29]) for limiting global warming to 2°C require that the world economy reach net-zero emissions in the 2060s. The corresponding emission pathways imply a carbon intensity of GDP that is lower than 0.07 kg per unit of GDP by 2040. However, scenarios consistent with achieving the goal of the Paris agreement to limit global warming to 1.5°C require net-zero emissions already by mid-century (Rogelj et al., 2018[14]) and thus steeper emission pathways.

Figure 5.2. Countries that increase their carbon pricing score also become more carbon efficient

Change of countries with respect to pricing all emissions at EUR 60 per tonne CO_2 and change in countries' carbon intensities of GDP

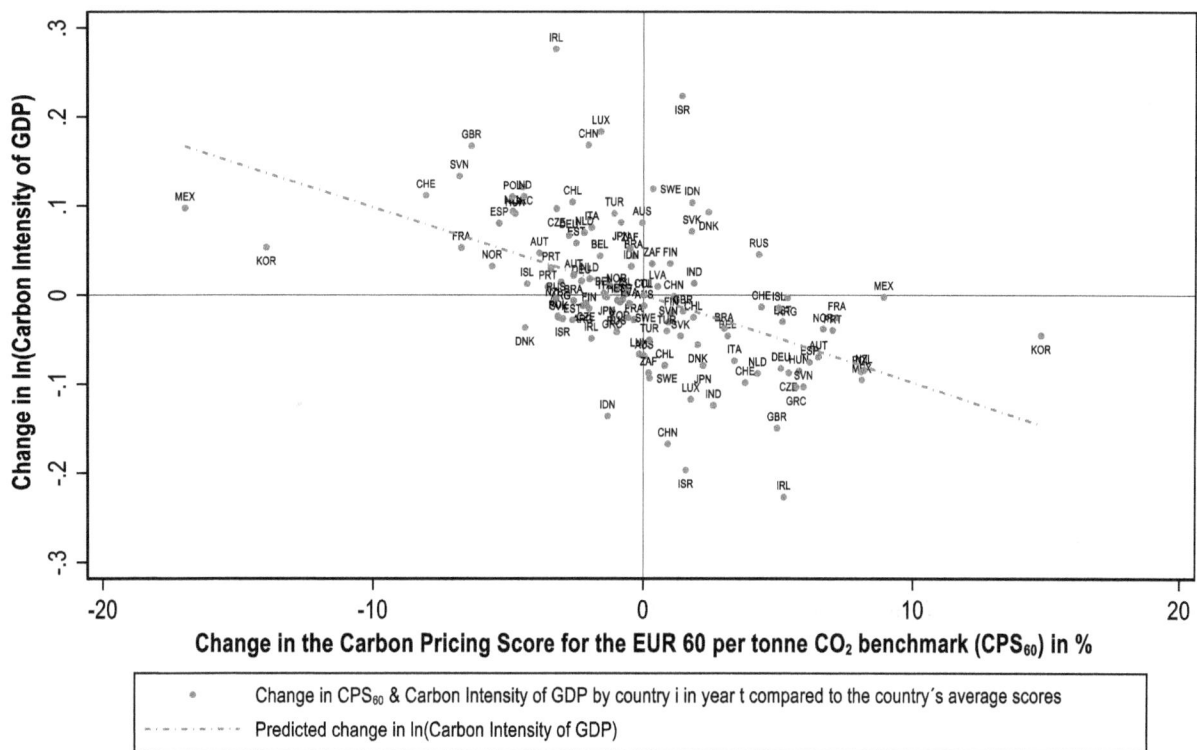

Reading Note: If a country increases its carbon pricing score (i.e. it moves towards the right), this goes hand in hand with a decrease of its carbon intensity of GDP (i.e. it moves downwards). The dotted line visualises the corresponding panel fixed effects regression of the carbon pricing score on the emission intensity of GDP.
Source: GDP data from the World Development Indicators (World Bank, 2020[28])

Economic output effects

Figure 5.3 shows that countries with a higher CPS are also generally richer, at least in terms of GDP per capita. Moreover, countries that increase their CPS (shown on the right side of Figure 5.4) increase their GDP per capita at the same time (shown in the upper half of Figure 5.4). These findings do not necessarily imply a direct causal effect in either direction. Countries with a high GDP per capita may find it easier to price carbon emissions, and the same may hold for countries becoming richer. However, the findings are also consistent with the notion that countries that employ carbon pricing as a key climate policy reduce emissions more economically, and thus benefit from superior economic performance.[1] With the Paris Agreement, countries decided to decarbonise their economies by about mid-century and given this commitment, those countries that decarbonise their economies more economically are likely to perform better across a broad range of dimensions including the level of GDP per capita.

Figure 5.3. Countries closer to the carbon pricing benchmark have a higher GDP per capita

GDP per capita and carbon pricing score in 2018

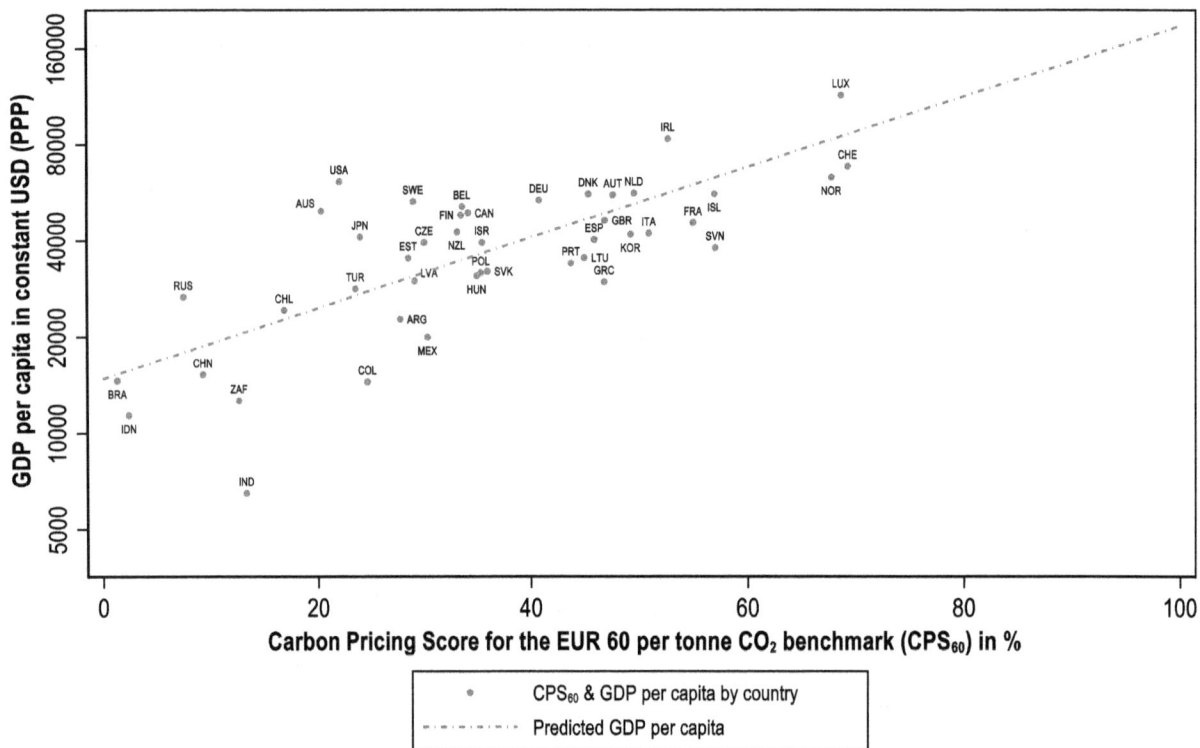

Reading Note: The graph shows that countries that have a higher carbon pricing score towards the benchmark of EUR 60 per tonne CO_2 (a low-end benchmark for carbon costs in 2030) have a higher GDP per capita.

Source: GDP data from the World Development Indicators (World Bank, 2020[28]).

Figure 5.4. Countries that progress more with carbon pricing show a stronger increase in GDP per capita

Change in countries´ progress towards pricing all emissions at least at EUR 60 per tonne CO2 and change in countries´ GDP per capita

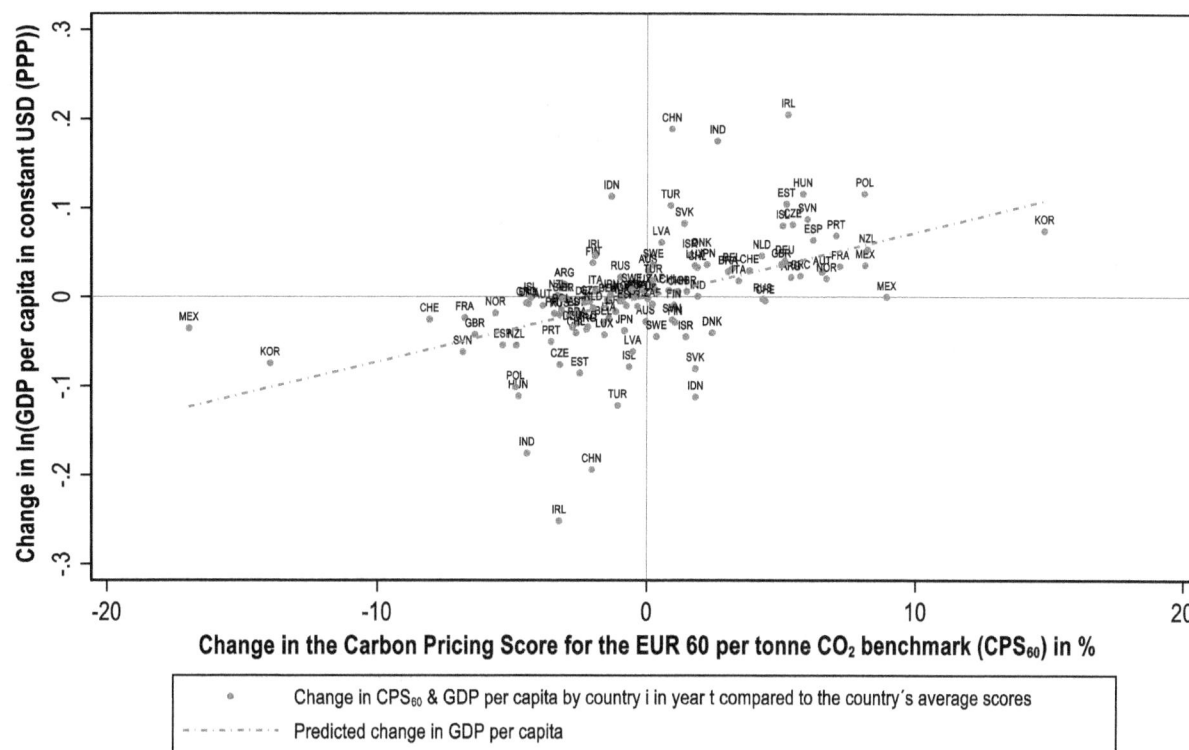

Change in the Carbon Pricing Score for the EUR 60 per tonne CO_2 benchmark (CPS_{60}) in %

•	Change in CPS_{60} & GDP per capita by country i in year t compared to the country's average scores
-------	Predicted change in GDP per capita

Note: If a country increases its progress towards pricing all its emissions at least at EUR 60 per tonne CO2 (i.e. it moves towards the right), GDP per capita increases (i.e. it moves upwards). The dotted line visualises the corresponding panel fixed effects regression of the carbon pricing score on GDP per capita.
Source: GDP per capita from the World Development Indicators (World Bank, 2020[28]).

References

Arlinghaus, J. (2015), "Impacts of Carbon Prices on Indicators of Competitiveness: A Review of Empirical Findings", *OECD Environment Working Papers*, No. 87, OECD Publishing, Paris, http://dx.doi.org/10.1787/5js37p21grzq-en. [1]

European Systemic Risk Board (2016), "Too late, too sudden: Transition to a low-carbon economy and systemic risk", *Reports of the Advisory Scientific Committee* 6, https://www.esrb.europa.eu/pub/pdf/asc/Reports_ASC_6_1602.pdf (accessed on 20 February 2018). [7]

Martin, R., M. Muûls and U. Wagner (2016), "The Impact of the European Union Emissions Trading Scheme on Regulated Firms: What Is the Evidence after Ten Years?", *Review of Environmental Economics and Policy*, Vol. 10/1, pp. 129-148, http://dx.doi.org/10.1093/reep/rev016. [2]

Peters, G. et al. (2017), "Key indicators to track current progress and future ambition of the Paris Agreement", *Nature Climate Change*, Vol. 7/2, pp. 118-122, http://dx.doi.org/10.1038/nclimate3202. [5]

Rogelj, J. et al. (2018), "Mitigation Pathways Compatible with 1.5°C in the Context of Sustainable Development", in Masson-Delmotte, V. et al. (eds.), *Global Warming of 1.5°C. An IPCC Special Report on the impacts of global warming of 1.5°C.*, IPCC. [6]

Sen, S. and H. Vollebergh (2018), "The effectiveness of taxing the carbon content of energy consumption", *Journal of Environmental Economics and Management*, Vol. 92, pp. 74-99, http://dx.doi.org/10.1016/J.JEEM.2018.08.017. [3]

Siegert, C. (ed.) (2020), *Mainstreaming the transition to a net-zero economy*, G30: Group of Thirty, Washington, D.C. [8]

World Bank (2020), *World Development Indicators*, World Bank, Washington, D.C:. [4]

Notes

[1] Carbon prices are key to cost-effective (or economic) emission reduction. They ensure that low-cost abatement options are carried out, before options that are more expensive are considered. Countries that heavily rely in policies other than carbon pricing likely miss out on some of the low-hanging abatement options and thus increase their overall abatement costs. Countries that delay abatement until it is unavoidable also risk increasing overall abatement costs as carbon-intensive capital can then become suddenly obsolete (European Systemic Risk Board (2016[33]); Siegert et al. (2020[35])).

Annex A. The permit price increase and the emission decrease in the EU ETS

From 2018 to 2019, permit prices in the European Union Emissions Trading System (EU ETS) increased by EUR 8.90 per tonne CO_2, from about EUR 16 to EUR 25 (ICAP, 2020[12]). At the same time, overall emissions in the EU ETS decreased by 8.9% (Marcu et al., 2020[13]), illustrating a significant short-term response of emitters covered by the EU ETS to higher permit prices. This Annex attempts to illustrate some important mechanisms behind the increase of permit prices and the reduction of emissions.

From a static theoretical perspective, the intersection of the marginal abatement cost curve with the emissions cap determines the permit price in a simple ETS without any price stability instruments. Observing a significant increase in permit price and emission reductions could be interpreted as a sign that cheap abatement options have been sufficient to fulfil the cap so far, but that now - with a more limited permit supply – more expensive abatement options need to be carried out. However, real world ETSs are considerably more complex than their simple theoretical counterparts. At least two dimensions are worth considering.

First, the cap is generally set for several years in advance according to a predetermined decreasing emission pathway. It is common to observe that caps are not binding in current trading periods. Observing positive permit prices can be interpreted as a sign that market participants believe that the cap will become binding some day in the future (when the permit supply will be more restricted). Observing an increase in permit prices would then be a sign that market participants expect more stringent climate policy in the future.

Second, many ETSs now include some form of price stability instruments (Flues and van Dender, 2020[23]). In case of the EU ETS, the Market Stability Reserve (MSR) injects permits into its reserve when the number of permits in free circulation (i.e. permits that emitters do not use for compliance with their obligation to surrender a number of permits equal to their emissions) exceeds a certain threshold. The MSR releases permits from its reserve when the number of permits in circulation falls below another (lower) threshold. In addition, when the number of permits in the reserve exceeds the number of permits auctioned in the previous year, the MSR cancels any permit in excess of the previous year´s auction volume. This automatic permit cancellation makes the cap endogenous, i.e. accompanying climate policies, which also reduce emissions, can cause an additional cap reduction (Perino, Ritz and van Benthem, 2019[30]).

What could explain the increase in permit prices and the decrease in emissions in the EU ETS in 2019? One answer is that the introduction of the MSR increased confidence in climate policy and the demand for permits given expectations of reduced permit supply in the future (Vivid Economics, 2020, p. 15[31]). This immediately increased permit prices. In response to higher permit prices, emitters in the EU ETS, and among those primarily utilities, cut emissions. For example, many utilities switched from emission intensive coal to burning natural gas (which is approximately half as emission-intensive as coal) for generating electricity, because higher permit prices made it more profitable to use gas instead of coal (Marcu et al., 2020, pp. 23-24[13]).

References

Flues, F. and K. van Dender (2020), "Carbon pricing design: Effectiveness, efficiency and feasibility: An investment perspective", *OECD Taxation Working Papers*, No. 48, OECD Publishing, Paris, https://dx.doi.org/10.1787/91ad6a1e-en. [3]

ICAP (2020), *International Carbon Action Partnership (ICAP) - ETS Prices*, https://icapcarbonaction.com/en/ets-prices (accessed on 13 October 2020). [1]

Marcu, A. et al. (2020), *2020 State of the EU ETS Report*, ERCST, Wegener Center, BloombergNEF and Ecoact. [2]

Perino, G., R. Ritz and A. van Benthem (2019), "Understanding Overlapping Policies: Internal Carbon Leakage and the Punctured Waterbed", *NBER Working Paper Series*, No. 25643, NBER, Cambridge, http://www.nber.org/papers/w25643.ack (accessed on 11 April 2019). [4]

Vivid Economics (2020), *Market stability measures*, Vivid Economics, London. [5]